# · A · Mammal · IS AN · Animal

## LIZZY ROCKWELL

HOLIDAY HOUSE  NEW YORK

# For Magnus

The publisher wishes to thank Louis N. Sorkin of the American Museum of Natural History
and Mark Omura of the Harvard University Museum of Comparative Zoology for their expert review of this book.

HOLIDAY HOUSE is registered in the U.S. Patent and Trademark Office.
Printed and Bound in November 2017 at Toppan Leefung, DongGuan City, China.
The artwork was created with ink and watercolor on Fabriano Artistico soft-press watercolor paper.
www.holidayhouse.com
First Edition
1 3 5 7 9 10 8 6 4 2
Library of Congress Cataloging-in-Publication Data

Names: Rockwell, Lizzy, author, illustrator.
Title: A mammal is an animal / Lizzy Rockwell.
Description: First edition. | New York : Holiday House, [2017]
Audience: Ages 4–8. | Audience: K to grade 3.
Identifiers: LCCN 2016048121 | ISBN 9780823436705 (hardcover)
Subjects: LCSH: Mammals—Juvenile literature.
Classification: LCC QL706.2 .R627 2017 | DDC 599—dc23
LC record available at https://lccn.loc.gov/2016048121

A mammal is an animal.

Animals are living things.
They can eat, breathe, move, and grow.

But is every animal a mammal?
**No!**

An earthworm is an animal.

It can eat, breathe, move, and grow.
But is an earthworm a mammal?

# No!
An earthworm is soft inside and out.

Common earthworm

Earthworms are a kind of
animal called an annelid.

A mammal has some
body parts that are hard.

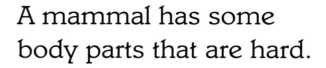

White-tailed
Male Deer

Hard parts inside
help this deer
stand and run.

Hard antlers

Hard hooves

9

Hard shell covers wings.

Hard shell covers legs.

Okay then, a ladybug is an animal.
A ladybug has body parts that are hard.
But is a ladybug a mammal?

**No!** Ladybugs are insects.
They have hard body parts
only on the outside.

There are many kinds of animals
that only have hard parts on the outside.
Not one of these is a mammal.

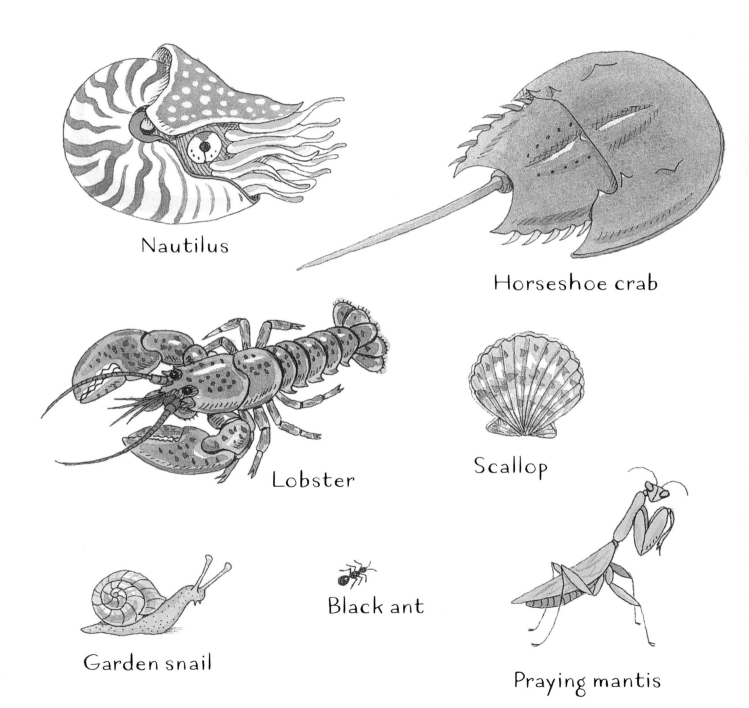

Nautilus

Horseshoe crab

Lobster

Scallop

Garden snail

Black ant

Praying mantis

A mammal is an animal with hard parts mostly on the inside. These hard parts are bones. They connect to make a skeleton. The long stack of bones down the middle make the spine. Those bones are called vertebrae.

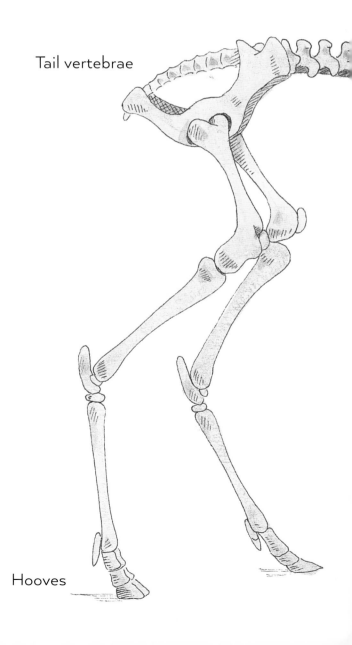

Tail vertebrae

Hooves

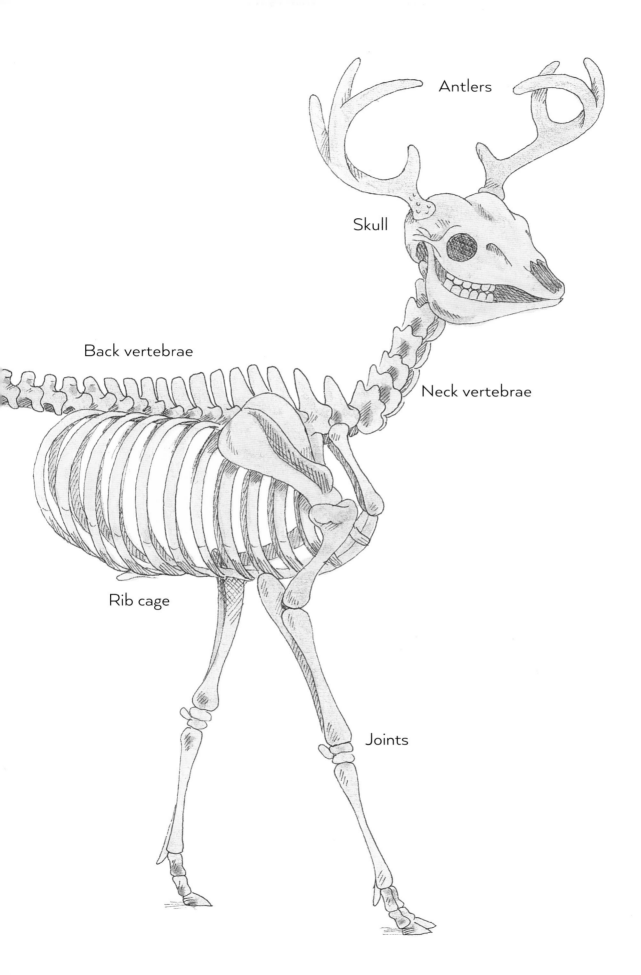

Antlers

Skull

Back vertebrae

Neck vertebrae

Rib cage

Joints

13

Okay, how about a sunfish?
A sunfish is an animal.

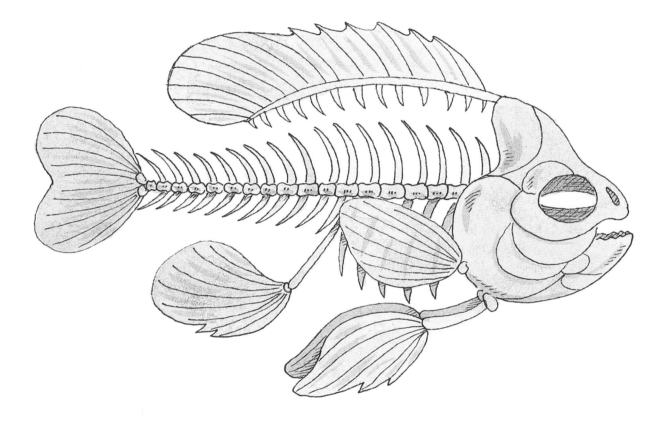

A sunfish has bones on the inside
with a long stack down the middle.
But is a sunfish a mammal?
**No!**

All animals need oxygen to breathe.

Mouth

Gills

Sunfish and other kinds of fish
get oxygen when water goes into
their mouths and through their gills.

A mammal gets oxygen when it breathes air into its lungs.

Harbor seals breathe air through their nostrils and mouth when above water.

Blowholes close under water.

This baby humpback whale holds its breath under water.

The **humpback whale**
breathes through two blowholes
on the top of its head.

Two lungs are
located inside
the whale's body.

The **harbor seal** holds
its breath under water.

Let's try this. A bullfrog is an animal.
A bullfrog breathes air into its lungs.
But is a bullfrog a mammal?
**No!**

Bullfrog

Nostrils for
breathing

# How about a garter snake?
## No!

Common garter snake

Snakes usually have
just one long lung.

Scales help reptiles
attract and store heat.

Frogs are amphibians and snakes are
reptiles. These animals are cold-blooded.
They need the heat of the sun, earth,
and water to keep warm.

A mammal can warm its body from the inside.
A mammal is warm-blooded.

Cardinal

Red fox

A mammal usually has fur or hair
to help it stay warm.

Okay, I've got it! A cardinal is an animal.
A cardinal can warm its body from the inside.
Instead of fur, feathers help keep it warm.
But is a cardinal a mammal?

Female cardinal

Male cardinal

**No!** A cardinal is a bird, and birds lay eggs. Baby birds grow inside the eggs. The mother and father keep those eggs warm in a nest. Baby birds hatch from the eggs.

Birds are the only animals that have feathers.

Snake eggs

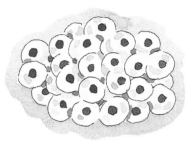

Frog eggs

Fish eggs

Spider egg sac

Skate egg purse

Ladybug eggs on a leaf

Earthworm eggs

Snakes, frogs, fish, spiders, clams,
insects, worms, and many other animals
lay eggs too.

Most mammals grow inside their mother's body in a place called the womb.

When it's time, the calf will be pushed through this birth canal.

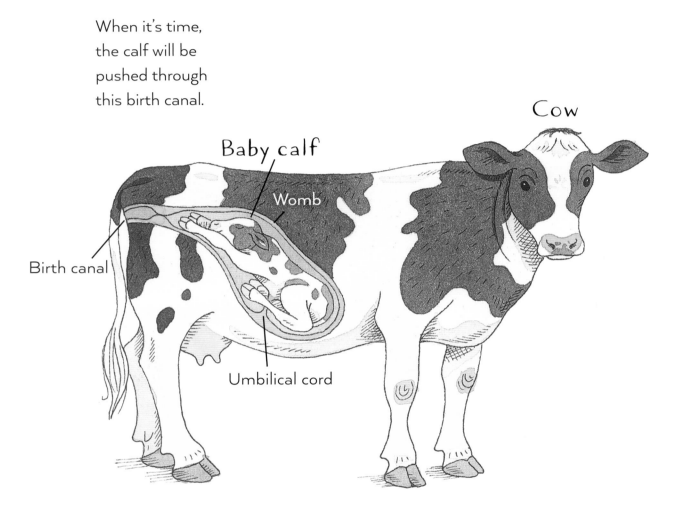

Cow

Baby calf

Womb

Birth canal

Umbilical cord

In the womb, the mammal baby gets oxygen and food from the mother's blood through a cord.

When a mammal baby is ready to be born,
it is pushed out of the mother's body.
The cord breaks away during birth,
and the baby takes his or her first breath of air.

A newborn mammal baby drinks only milk.
The milk comes right out of the mother's body.

Teat

Cow's udder

The mammal baby suckles the milk and grows and grows and grows until it can eat all kinds of food on its own.

Two-month-old calf

Young mammals stay close to their parents for months or years and learn from them.

White-headed capuchin monkeys

Red kangaroos

Pigs

Bottlenose dolphins

African elephants

Mammals sure are amazing animals.

# HEY, YOU ARE ONE TOO!

# SOME STRANGE MAMMALS

## MONOTREMES LAY EGGS!

There are just three kinds of monotremes: the duck-billed platypus, the short-beaked echidna, and the long-beaked echidna.

The **duck-billed platypus**
lays eggs in a nest underground.
She keeps them warm with her body.

The **short-beaked echidna**
keeps her eggs under a flap on her belly.

A **baby echidna**
is called a puggle.

These strange mammals lay one or two leathery eggs, around the size of a marble. When the eggs hatch the babies sip milk that oozes from the mother's skin.

## MARSUPIALS HAVE POUCHES!

There are more than 250 kinds of marsupials.
A mother marsupial gives birth to tiny furless babies.
These babies are too fragile to live outside.

A mother koala
and her joey

A Virginia opossum can
have up to 13 babies at one time.

A gray kangaroo joey
will stop visiting the pouch after
about a year.

The newborn babies crawl to a pouch in front of the mother's belly.
They find teats for suckling milk. After a while they are strong and furry
and can come and go from the pouch. A baby marsupial is called a joey.

# MAMMAL FACTS

## ALL MAMMALS:

Drink milk.

Breathe air.

Have a skeleton and a spine.

Are warm-blooded.

Stay with their parents when
young and learn from them.

## MOST MAMMALS:

Develop inside the mother's body in the womb and
are born alive and ready for the world outside.

Breathe through their nostrils and mouth.

Have fur or hair.

Have two or four legs.

## SOME MAMMALS:

Like whales and dolphins, breathe air through a blowhole on top of
their heads and live only in water. Instead of legs, they have a tail
and flippers.

Like kangaroos and koalas, are born too small and weak to survive in
the outside world. They crawl into the mother's pouch and drink
milk till they are strong and protected by a fur coat.

Like strange platypus and echidnas, are hatched from eggs.

Like bats, can fly.

## ONE KIND OF MAMMAL:

Walks upright on two legs.

Uses words to communicate.

Wears clothing.

Can make up stories and pictures.

Can build houses and machines.

Guess who?

* The answer is on page 33.

## REFERENCE SOURCES

*Smithsonian Natural History: The Ultimate Guide to Everything on Earth*
Copyright 2012, Dorling Kindersley Limited

*Smithsonian Animal: The Definitive Visual Guide*
Copyright 2011, Dorling Kindersley Limited

*Mammals: A Guide to Familiar American Species*
A Golden Nature Guide
by Herbert S. Zim, Ph.D., and Donald F. Hoffmeister, Ph.D.
Illustrated by James Gordon Irving
Copyright 1955, Golden Press

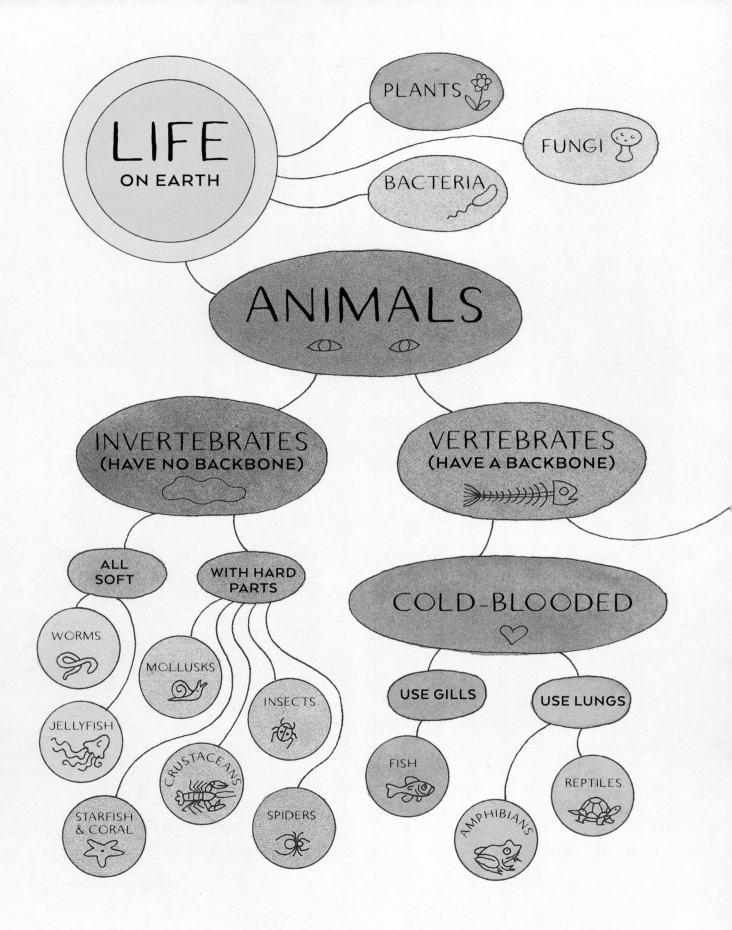

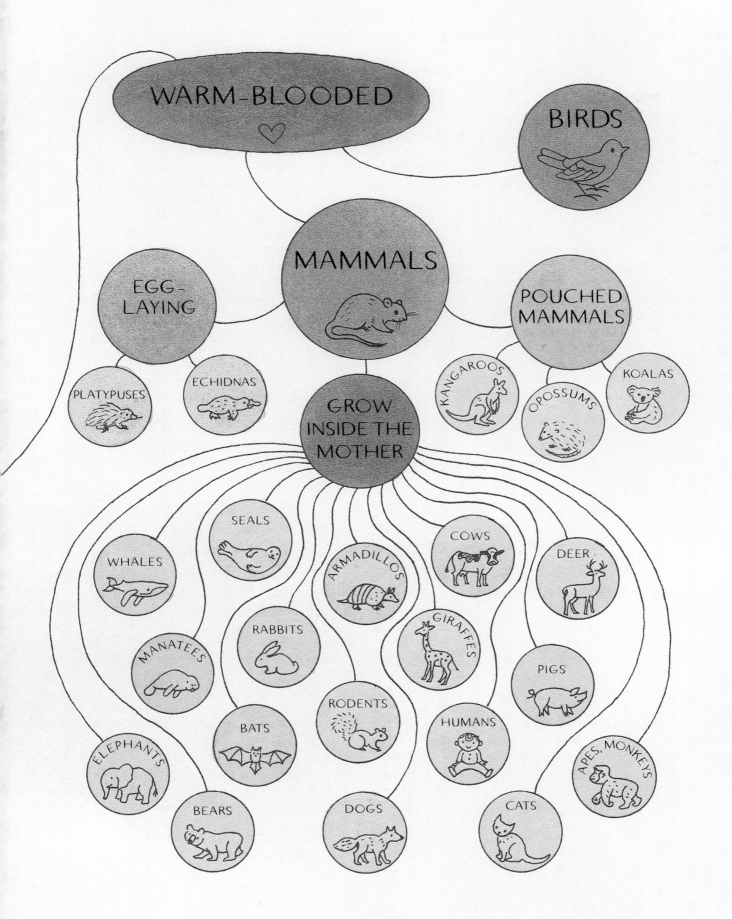